MOCKTAILS

NEW HOLLAND

MOCKTAILS

DAVID BIGGS

First published in 2006 by
New Holland Publishers (UK) Ltd
London • Cape Town • Sydney • Auckland
Text and photographs copyright © 2005
New Holland Publishers (UK) Ltd
Copyright © 2006 New Holland Publishers (UK) Ltd

Garfield House
86–88 Edgware Road
London W2 2EA
www.newhollandpublishers.com

Level 1, Unit 4
14 Aquatic Drive
Frenchs Forest, NSW 2086
Australia

80 McKenzie Street
Cape Town 8001
South Africa

218 Lake Road
Northcote
Auckland
New Zealand

ISBN 1-84537-627-7

SENIOR EDITOR: Corinne Masciocchi
DESIGN CONCEPT: Christelle Marais
DESIGNER: Rod Teasdale
PHOTOGRAPHY: Stuart West
FOOD STYLING: Stella Murphy
PRODUCTION: Marion Storz
EDITORIAL DIRECTION: Rosemary Wilkinson

Reproduction by Pica Digital PTE Ltd, Singapore
Printed and bound by Tien Wah Press, Malaysia

1 3 5 7 9 10 8 6 4 2

CONTENTS

INTRODUCTION

An ever-increasing number of people are realising that it's not necessary to get drunk in order to have fun. There are many good reasons not to want alcohol at a party, the most obvious one is that you want to remain sober to drive yourself and your friends home safely and legally after the party.

Pregnant women may also want to limit their alcohol intake, while others choose to abstain altogether and some subscribe to religions that forbid the use of alcohol. For whatever reason you may prefer your drinks without alcohol, this book offers you a wide range of alcohol-free cocktails to provide an evening of drinking pleasure without the usual morning-after headache.

It seems we live such rushed lives these days that we don't even have time to relax with a leisurely drink any more. It can sometimes seem like everybody just wants to pour as much alcohol down their throats in as little time as possible.

It's hard to imagine an activity more wasteful and senseless than binge drinking. You spend a great deal of money getting unconscious and wake up the next day feeling awful. And your money is gone.

Non-alcoholic cocktails, also known as 'virgin' drinks, or 'mocktails', don't have to be boring or tasteless. A clever host will know how to balance flavours to create an exciting drink, whether it's intoxicating or not. This balance consists of matching sweet flavours with acidity, or savoury flavours with fruitiness. Think of

some of the balances of flavour that have become traditional in food: pork is often served with apple jelly, duck with orange, and turkey with cranberry sauce. The reason cola has become the best selling beverage in the world is because it consists of exactly the right combination of sweetness and acidity.

This book offers a range of recipes without giving exact quantities for each ingredient. The reason for this is that each country has its own measures for drinks – some use fluid ounces while others use centilitres, and still others use traditional measures like jiggers, gills and pints. Here we use proportions wherever possible – one part of this to two parts of that. This also has the advantage that you can mix enough for a single drink or make a whole batch to serve a crowd. The recipes should be regarded as guidelines and can be altered and adjusted to suit your own tastes.

Remember that a good drink is one that appeals to all the senses. It should look good, smell good, taste good and even sound good, as the ice tinkles against the edges of the glass.

Shaken or stirred?

The difference between a great drink and an indifferent one often depends on attention to small details. You could, of course, simply bung all the ingredients of a mocktail into a jug, stir them about a bit and pour them into the nearest glass. You'd end up with a drink, but it wouldn't be particularly interesting, or attractive. This is why each

recipe includes instructions on how to treat the ingredients to bring out the best in them.

Some drinks recipes call for the ingredients to be shaken, blended or gently stirred. And sometimes a cocktail recipe will tell you the drink should be 'built' (or layered). So, why the difference?

It's all a matter of getting the ingredients combined correctly. A cocktail shaker with a few ice cubes in it ensures the contents are not only thoroughly combined, but chilled while also slightly diluting the contents. For best results, the drink should be shaken quite vigorously. A famous bartender is quoted as saying 'Shake the thing! You're not trying to rock it to sleep!'.

The cheerful rattle of a cocktail shaker adds an essential beat to any party. Drinks that contain a fizzy ingredient, like soda water or ginger ale, are not shaken, as this would result in an explosive mess. This is why these recipes always tell you to mix the rest of the ingredients first, then add the carbonated component and stir gently – just enough to combine the ingredients evenly without losing the bubbles.

Drinks that include semi-solid ingredients, such as soft fruit, ice cream or egg, are best mixed in an electric blender that quickly turns the components into a homogenous, creamy texture. And when you want the ingredients to remain slightly separate so that the drinker is provided with a series of consecutive flavour experiences rather than one flavour throughout, you are instructed to build the drink, adding one ingredient carefully on top of the previous one.

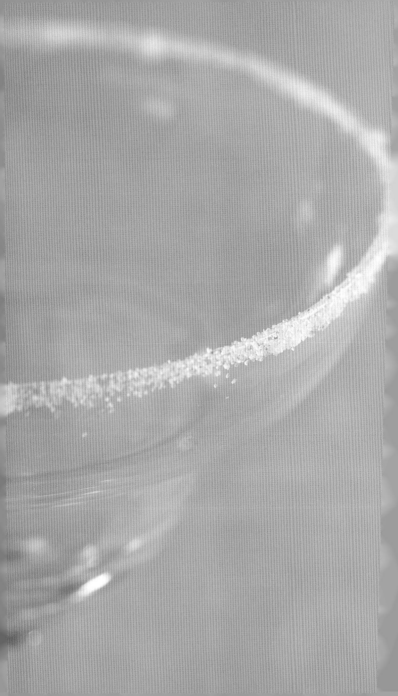

EQUIPMENT

Whether you find your pleasure in skydiving, golf, jogging or mixing drinks, you'll need some basic equipment to get you started.

It's not always necessary to surround yourself with all the latest hi-tech gizmos – unless you are a full-time professional – but a few basic tools will increase your enjoyment and make things easier. Stores that stock bar supplies will offer you all manner of blenders, shakers, strainers, squeezers and crushers, all of which are fun to use. But for an occasional party with friends, a few simple tools will suffice.

You probably have some of them in your kitchen already. It makes life so much more pleasant for you and your guests if all your equipment is set out in readiness before they arrive. Good preparation makes all the difference. Below are some of the tools you'll find useful.

Chopping board

This comes in handy for cutting fruit on for your drinks. A wooden board makes cutting easy and protects the knife blade and your work surface.

Bar knife

Any smallish, very sharp knife will do here. You'll find it handy for cutting neat slices of lemon, dicing fruit and slitting the foil on bottle necks.

Bar measure

Although exact quantities are not specified in most of the recipes in this book, it's handy to have a bar measure available. It does make it easier to pour consistent quantities. Probably the most useful measure is one with two cups fixed bottom to bottom and fitted with a handle. Alternatively, you can use a shot glass or egg cup.

Cocktail shaker

Useful for blending ingredients, particularly those of different consistencies, like cream and fruit juice. A few cubes of ice inside act as beaters and slightly dilute the ingredients. Cocktail shakers are usually fitted with strainers, so you can pour the drink while keeping the ice cubes behind.

Blender

This is a valuable piece of bar equipment that makes nice smooth milkshakes and can be used to turn soft fruits like bananas and peaches into a creamy-textured purée in a few seconds. It's worth investing in one because you'll find plenty of use for it in your kitchen.

Ice bucket and tongs

Almost all mocktails call for ice in one form or another. You could always use a mixing bowl from the kitchen, of course, but an ice bucket keeps the ice cold and looks good on the bar.

Ice crusher

Many drinks call for crushed ice, so if you're going to be reasonably serious about your mocktails, a manual or electric ice crusher is a great help. The alternative is to place ice cubes in a bag or linen tea towel and smack them with a meat tenderising hammer. Some hosts prefer to whack the ice bag against a wall to crush the ice. A little dramatic and not elegant, but it does work after a fashion!

Assorted jugs and bowls

You need a selection of bowls and jugs (preferably with an ice-guard) to store supplies of iced water, fruit juices, milk and cream. You don't want to have to rush out to the kitchen every time you need another glass of water.

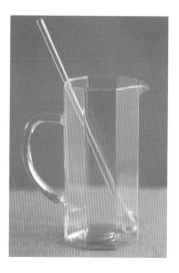

Frosted glasses

Some drinks call for frosted glasses. To achieve this, have a saucer of caster sugar handy, run a slice of lemon or orange around the rim of the glass to moisten it, then dip it into the saucer so that the sugar sticks to the damp rim. In the case of savoury drinks, salt can be used instead of sugar and the rim dampened with one of the drink's ingredients instead of lemon juice. If you plan to serve a number of drinks in frosted glasses, they can be prepared in advance and stored in the refrigerator. The more preparation a good host does ahead of the party, the less stressful the event will be. And ideally, the host should have as much fun as the guests!

Glasses

Mocktail recipes always call for particular styles of glass – highball glasses, lowball glasses, Martini glasses, Champagne flutes, wine glasses, and so on. It's really not necessary to have them all, unless you're running a professional bar. You'll get by perfectly well with a selection consisting of wine glasses, tall cylindrical glasses and shortish (whisky) glasses. If you do become more serious, the traditional Martini glass is an attractive addition. For short drinks, or 'shooters' you could add little shot glasses to your collection.

Tea towels

No matter how tidy you are, serving drinks can be a damp activity. Have a few small, clean tea towels handy to mop up spills and dry hands and glasses.

Stirring spoon

A slim, long-handled bar spoon is good to have around. It reaches right to the bottom of tall glasses or jugs for mess-free stirring.

Nutmeg grater

This is not a must, but does add a touch of professionalism. You can, of course, buy your nutmeg ready grated. A small grater can also be useful for grating chocolate over a milk-based drink.

Cocktail sticks

Many drinks call for a cherry or olive as a garnish. You can spear these on ordinary wooden toothpicks or use special party cocktail sticks sometimes decorated with a little frilly top.

Vegetable peeler

You probably have one of these already. It's handy for peeling thin strips of lemon or arrange zest from the fruit. If you're going to be serious about virgin cocktails, it's worth buying a zester, which takes very neat, thin strips of zest from the skin of an orange or lemon.

INGREDIENTS

Unless yours is a professional bar, you can't be expected to stock every available drink used in mocktails. Rather keep a few basic ingredients on hand, so you can balance sweet with sour and bitter, and savoury with fruit. The following list is just a suggestion and should enable you to create a good range of different drinks. Keep an eye open in supermarkets for interesting fruit syrups or toppings. It's amazing what you can use to create exciting mocktails.

Bitters

There is a whole range of bitters, all used to add a touch of bitterness to an otherwise too-sweet drink. The best known is called Angostura bitters. While actually an alcoholic liquid, Angostura bitters is usually used so sparingly that the amount of alcohol it adds to any drink is negligible. If you're drinking a non-alcoholic drink because you're driving later, or for health reasons, the addition of a few drops of bitters will really not harm you. If, however, you are abstaining from alcohol for religious reasons, or from strong moral objections, you'd be better off avoiding bitters and substituting fresh lime juice. You can also find various commercial bitters that do not contain alcohol.

Caster sugar

This fine white sugar, often used in baking, is ideal for sweetening drinks because it dissolves more easily than granulated sugar.

Egg

While some drinkers shudder at the thought of swallowing raw egg, it can add a delicious texture to any cocktail. Egg yolk gives a drink a velvet creaminess, while the white of an egg, shaken into a drink, lends it a silvery sheen that's very pretty. Eggs should be as fresh as they come and drinks containing raw egg yolk or egg white should be avoided by pregnant women and the elderly.

Fruit purée

Very useful to have when you're making cocktails, and easy to make in a blender. Simply place bananas, strawberries, ripe peaches or watermelon chunks in the blender and whiz them to a smooth, creamy consistency. Fruit should be peeled, and any hard stones or pips should be removed before blending.

Glacé cherries

These are cherries that have been candied, giving them a bright red, glossy shine. This is done by soaking them in sugar syrup until the sugar replaces the moisture, thus extending their storage qualities. They are widely available from all good supermarkets. No good mocktail should be without!

Gomme

A sugar syrup used to sweeten drinks. A solution of sugar and water, it's easy to make your own (see Sugar syrup, page 23).

tea towel, and smack it with a hammer or rolling pin.

Add an exciting finishing touch to any drink with flavoured ice. Freeze an ice tray of undiluted lemon juice, lime juice or other fruit juice as an attractive and flavourful addition to a drink. You can also create mint ice cubes by placing a mint leaf in each section of the ice tray, covering it with water and freezing it.

Grenadine

A sweet red flavouring syrup made from pomegranate juice. It adds delicate sweetness and a pretty pink colour to a drink.

Ice

Ice is a vital ingredient of every mocktail – warm mocktails are simply not acceptable. You should have a generous supply of ice cubes as well as crushed ice. If no ice crusher is available, place a cup of ice cubes in a tea towel and bash it against the wall to shatter the ice. You can also place it on a hard surface, in a

Orgeat

A sweet syrup with a distinctive almond flavour. Used for adding sweetness and nuttiness.

Sirop de cassis

A non-alcoholic syrup made from blackcurrants. Useful for adding colour and flavour to drinks.

Sour mix

Sour mix adds a clean, sour tang to any drink. Make it in advance and keep it in the fridge.

Squeeze about six large lemons into a jar or cocktail shaker, add an equal quantity of water, two tablespoons of caster sugar and the white of one egg. Shake well and set aside until needed. (Any liquid containing egg should not be stored for more than a couple of days and should not be ingested by pregnant women and the elderly.)

Sugar syrup

The simplest way of adding sweetness to a drink is to have a bottle or jug of prepared sugar syrup. It's easy to make. Heat two parts of sugar and one part of water in a saucepan and stir until the sugar has dissolved. Allow to cool and store in a suitable bottle, ready for use. It can be kept for at least a week before the sugar starts to crystallise.

Syrups, various

You can find a whole range of flavoured syrups in your local supermarket, often marketed as ice cream toppings. It helps to add variety to have a few of these in your bar store. Chocolate syrup is useful, as are the various fruit- and berry-flavoured syrups.

Tabasco sauce

This hot sauce is made with three ingredients: red pepper, high-grain vinegar and a small amount of salt. Use it sparingly to add a kick to savoury mocktails.

Worcestershire sauce

Also known as Worcester sauce, this dark brown condiment is widely used in both dishes and drinks. Vinegar, chilli peppers, soy sauce and anchovies are among its many ingredients. It is a main ingredient of Bloody Mary and the non-alcoholic version, Virgin Mary.

TALK THE TALK

Every human activity, from hang-gliding to hunting and from bowls to book-keeping, has its own vocabulary. You don't necessarily have to know every word in the book, but it does help to be able to toss in the occasional correct word or phrase, just to show you know what you're doing.

The same, of course, applies to cocktail mixing – alcoholic or not. You can always say something like, 'bung in some of that yellow stuff', but it sounds a lot more professional to say 'float a little Galliano on the surface'. The following list of cocktail terms might come in handy, especially if you want to impress your sophisticated friends with your familiarity with cocktail talk.

Aperitif a drink served before a meal, usually with a dryish flavour, to stimulate the appetite.

Blending ingredients with different textures, like fruit, ice and juice, can be mixed to a smooth consistency by placing them in an electric blender and running it for a few seconds. An effective way of achieving a homogenous mixture.

Build to 'build' a drink, one ingredient is poured directly on top of the previous one in the glass, and not stirred, so you have layers of flavours that greet the drinker one by one.

Cup a measure sometimes referred to in this book. Not an exact quantity, although the official American cup contains 8 fluid ounces of liquid. The metric cup contains 250 ml. For the purposes of cocktail mixing, use an ordinary tea cup. Size is immaterial.

Dash a dash is a small splash, usually used to denote the quantity of strongly flavoured ingredients, like bitters or lime juice.

Digestif a drink served at the end of a meal, in order to settle the digestion. Usually fairly sweet, like a port or liqueur.

Flip a flip is a drink made with an egg as a main ingredient. Usually smooth and creamy in texture and rich in flavour.

Float a) a drink made by adding a scoop of ice cream on the top of a glass of carbonated drink (usually a cola).

b) the method of adding an ingredient very carefully on the previous layer of the cocktail so the colours are perfectly separated. The best way to float one ingredient on to another is to pour it slowly over the back of a spoon into the glass.

Frosting the rim of a glass can be 'frosted' with sugar or salt, by moistening it with lemon juice or one of the ingredients of the drink, then pressing it into a saucer of caster sugar or salt, so that the grains stick to the damp glass rim. The effect is very attractive, as well as adding flavour and texture to the drink.

Garnish any solid ingredient used to decorate a cocktail. This could be a cherry on a cocktail stick, or a slice of fruit placed over the rim of the glass. Other common garnishes include cocktail olives, strawberries, celery stalks (for drinks like the Virgin Mary), fresh mint sprigs and twists of citrus peel (see Twist). A garnish should ideally be simple, and always edible. Paper parasols are best avoided!

Ice an essential ingredient for cocktails. Purists insist that ice should never be used more than once, and the most fussy bartenders claim that ice made in a domestic fridge freezes too slowly and is too 'wet' for cocktail use. They prefer professionally made flash-frozen ice, which lasts longer and melts slowly.

Jigger a small measure used by professional barmen to obtain the correct amount of liquid. Similar to the 'pony' (see Pony), containing roughly three tablespoons of liquid.

Muddle some ingredients, particularly combinations of dry and wet (like mint or herbs and soda water) are 'muddled together' by crushing them with the back of a spoon or special muddler.

Neat a drink is served 'neat' when it has no ice or mixer added to it.

Pony an American cocktail measure containing 30 ml (1 fl oz) of liquid, or roughly two tablespoons.

Punch a large party drink, usually made in a bowl or basin, in quantities large enough to serve a whole party. Proper punch bowls come equipped with matching cups for serving the drinks.

Rocks (on the) when a drink is described as 'on the rocks' it has been poured over a glass of ice cubes in the glass in which it is served.

Scoop an ice scoop is a handy utensil for transferring ice cubes or crushed ice from the ice bucket to the glass. Not any particular size, but usually containing about half a cup.

Shaken this refers to a drink that is mixed by placing it in a cocktail shaker with ice cubes, and then shaken vigorously before being strained into a cocktail glass.

Stirred this is the method used to mix ingredients when not too much brisk shaking is required. Usually used when one of the ingredients is carbonated (eg. soda water) in order to retain the bubbles.

Twist a twist is a longish strip of peel (usually lemon or orange) twisted into a pretty shape and dropped into a drink. This has two results: it adds flavour and aroma; and enhances the appearance of a drink.

Zest the oily aromatic substance that is found in the outer layer of citrus peel. By twisting a little lemon peel over a drink you spray it with the fresh zest aroma.

Recipes

Colourful, tasty, great-looking drinks
that can be made in minutes!

Appleade

This is a pleasant, subtle-flavoured summer drink that can be made a day or two ahead of time and set aside in the fridge until needed.

2 large green apples, cut into small cubes
Boiling water (enough to cover the apple cubes)
1 Tbsp brown sugar
Crushed ice
Pinch of ground cinnamon
Slice of apple, to garnish

Place the apple pieces in a bowl and pour the boiling water over them. Add the sugar and stir to dissolve. Leave to cool, strain, then chill the liquid until needed. Discard the apple pieces. To serve, fill a cocktail glass with crushed ice, pour the appleade over it, dust lightly with ground cinnamon and garnish with a slice of apple.

Cranberry Sparkler

Cranberry juice is becoming increasingly popular as a pleasantly tangy fruit drink, usually with just enough acidity to make it exciting.

Crushed ice
1 part cranberry juice
1 part fresh lemon juice
1 part soda water
Slice of lemon, to garnish

Fill a highball glass with **crushed ice** and pour the **cranberry** and **lemon juices**, and **soda water** over it. Stir gently. Garnish with a **slice of lemon**.

Pussyfoot

I am told that this citrus-based drink is an excellent
cure for hangovers. Make sure the egg
is very fresh. This drink is best avoided by pregnant
women and the elderly.

Ice cubes
1 part fresh lemon juice
1 part fresh orange juice
1 part lime juice
Splash of grenadine
1 egg yolk
Maraschino cherry, to garnish

Place five or six ice cubes in a cocktail shaker
and add the lemon, orange and lime juices
along with the grenadine and the egg yolk.
Shake well until the mixture is blended. Strain into
a chilled wine glass and garnish with a cherry.

Cinderella

I suppose this drink should ideally be drunk
from a glass slipper, but they're not
easy to find these days.

Ice cubes
1 part tinned pineapple juice
1 part fresh lemon juice
1 part fresh orange juice
Dash of grenadine
Soda water
Slice of pineapple, to garnish

Place five or six ice cubes in a cocktail shaker
and pour in the pineapple, lemon and
orange juices, and grenadine. Shake well and
strain into a tall glass. Top up with soda water
and garnish with a slice of pineapple.

Dry Grape Cocktail

For a drink that's not stickily sweet, try this elegant cocktail. The grenadine adds colour and can be used to adjust the sweetness to taste.

Crushed ice
2 parts white grape juice
1 part fresh lemon juice
Splash of grenadine

Place a scoop of **crushed ice** in a cocktail shaker. Add the **grape** and **lemon juices** and the **grenadine** to taste. Shake well and strain into a cocktail glass.

Cranberry Cooler

This is a slightly different version of the Cranberry Sparkler (see page 33), using lime cordial instead of the lemon juice, and ginger ale in place of the soda water.

Crushed ice
1 part cranberry juice
Splash of lime cordial
1 part ginger ale
Slice of lemon, to garnish

Fill a highball glass with **crushed ice** and pour the **cranberry juice, lime cordial** and **ginger ale** over it. Stir gently. Garnish with a **slice of lemon**.

Lime Cola

To give a sophisticated zing to a cola drink,
add a little fresh lime juice.

Crushed ice
1 lime
Cola

Fill a tall glass with **crushed ice**. Cut the **lime**
in half and squeeze the juice over the ice.
Top up with **cola** and stir gently.

Pony's Neck

A non-alcoholic version of the old favourite Horse's Neck, some claim it's better than the original!

Dash of Angostura bitters

1 orange

1 lemon

Crushed ice

Dash of lime cordial

Ginger ale

Maraschino or glacé cherry

Shake a dash of **bitters** into a tall glass and swirl to coat the sides. Peel the **orange** to make a thin, unbroken spiral. Hook this over the edge of a tall glass, so that it forms a spiral into the glass. Squeeze half the **orange** and the **lemon** into a separate glass, with a scoop of **crushed ice**. Add the **lime cordial** and stir well. Strain into the prepared glass and top with **ginger ale**. Decorate with a **cherry** on a stick and serve.

Lime Cooler

When you're looking for a drink that is not sweet, this could be the one.

Ice cubes
1 Tbsp lime juice
Tonic water
Slice of lime, to garnish

Fill a tall glass with ice cubes and pour over the lime juice. Top up with tonic water, stir gently and garnish with a slice of lime.

Lime Rickey

'Lime and soda' is one of the oldest non-alcoholic cocktail drinks for adults. This version has the added sophistication of a dash of grenadine.

Ice cubes
1 part lime cordial
Soda water
Dash of grenadine
Sprig of mint, to garnish

Fill a tall glass with ice cubes. Pour in the lime cordial, top up with soda water, add a dash of grenadine and stir gently. A sprig of mint adds a nice touch and aroma.

Cranberry Grape Cocktail

The slight tartness of cranberry juice is just enough
to offset the sweetness of grape juice.
You may like to add a squeeze of lemon juice
to the blend if it's too sweet for your palate.

Crushed ice
1 part cranberry juice
1 part white grape juice
Squeeze of lemon juice (optional)
Mint leaf, to garnish

Fill a Champagne flute with crushed ice,
pour over the cranberry and grape juices,
and the lemon juice, if using. Stir well and
garnish with a mint leaf.

Fun-Gria

Sangria is usually made with red wine and orange juice. This version uses red grape juice to replace the wine, and the result is a very exciting drink!

Lemon juice and caster sugar, for frosting
Ice cubes
1 part fresh orange juice
1 part red grape juice
Generous squeeze of lemon juice
Orange zest
Slice of lemon, to garnish

Rub the rim of a large wine glass with lemon juice then dip it into a saucer of caster sugar to frost the rim. Place four ice cubes in a shaker, add the orange and grape juices and the lemon juice. Shake well and strain into the frosted glass. Add a sprinkling of orange zest and garnish with a slice of lemon.

Shirley Temple

Named after the legendary child actress, this drink was originally designed for children. Many adults have discovered they enjoy it too!

Ice cubes
2 dashes of grenadine
Ginger ale
Slice of orange and maraschino cherry, to garnish

Fill a tall glass with ice cubes, splash in the grenadine, then top up with ginger ale. Garnish with a slice of orange and a cherry. If you find it too sweet, stir in a squeeze of fresh lime juice, too.

Virgin Manhattan

The word 'virgin' applied to any cocktail indicates that it does not contain alcohol. You can turn many cocktails into virgins simply by leaving out the alcohol.

Ice cubes
1 part cranberry juice
1 part fresh orange juice
Dash of maraschino cherry syrup
Splash of lemon juice
Dash of Angostura bitters
Maraschino cherry, to garnish

Place six ice cubes in a cocktail shaker, then add all the ingredients except for the cherry. Shake well and strain into a cocktail glass. Garnish with a cherry on a cocktail stick.

Virgin Mary

As the name suggests, this is the ever popular Bloody Mary, but without the vodka.

Ice cubes
1 can tomato juice
2 Tbsp fresh lemon juice
2 dashes of Worcestershire sauce
2 drops of Tabasco sauce
Pinch of celery salt
Salt and pepper, to taste
Celery stick

Place a scoop of **ice cubes** in a cocktail shaker, then add all the ingredients, except for the celery stick, and shake well. Strain into a lowball glass and use the **celery stick** as a stirrer.

Grape Crush

We are fortunate these days to be able to buy
a wide range of pure fruit juices in cartons,
cans or bottles, so fruit-based drinks
can be enjoyed all year round.

Crushed ice
3 parts grape juice
1 part cranberry juice
1 part sour mix (see page 23)
Lemonade

Fill a wine glass with crushed ice, add the
grape and cranberry juices along with
the sour mix and stir well. Top up with
lemonade and serve.

Wimbledon Winner

Anybody who follows tennis will know that Wimbledon and strawberries and cream are an inseparable match. This drink is the perfect accompaniment to an afternoon watching the finals on TV. You can vary quantities to suit your taste (and pocket).

Dozen fresh strawberries, rInsed and hulled
Enough single cream to cover the strawberries
1 Tbsp caster sugar
Generous pinch of powdered ginger
Soda water
Ice cubes

Place the **strawberries, cream, sugar** and **ginger** in a blender and combine them to a smooth consistency. Pour the blend into a jug, add **soda water** to almost fill the jug and a generous helping of **ice cubes**. Sir well before serving.

Banana Bomb

This delicious drink was originally devised as an instant breakfast for my children, who were always in too much of a hurry to catch the school bus to have time for a regular meal. They could gulp and run — and they never knew they'd had raw egg! Pregnant women and the elderly should not be served this drink.

1 ripe banana
1 whole egg
1 Tbsp runny honey
Enough chilled whole milk to fill the glass

Cut the **banana** into chunks and place in a blender. Add the **egg**, **honey** and **milk**, and blend to a smooth milkshake consistency. Serve in a tall glass. (For those who hesitate at the thought of including a raw egg, this can be omitted, although it does reduce the richness.)

Black Cow

This is a popular version of the 'float' theme,
especially in America, where root beer is far more
readily available than it is elsewhere.

2 scoops vanilla ice cream
Root beer, well chilled

Place the ice cream in a tall glass, pour the
root beer over it and serve with a thick
straw and long-handled spoon.

Chocolate Fizz

This drink adds a slight sparkle to the ordinary chocolate milk drink. It's also less filling than a milkshake.

2 generous Tbsp chocolate syrup
Cold whole milk
Soda water

Pour the **chocolate syrup** into a tall glass, add the **milk** to about two thirds of the glass, and stir until all the chocolate has dissolved. Top up with **soda water** and stir gently again before serving.

Chocolate Almond Shake

Chocolate and nut flavours are natural companions, hence the large number of chocolate bars that contain nuts. They combine just as well in a drink. This one is particularly rich and decadent and makes a good dessert when the ice is omitted.

Crushed ice
1 part chocolate syrup
1 part almond syrup
4 parts single cream
Maraschino cherry, to garnish

Place a scoop of **crushed ice** in a cocktail shaker and add the **chocolate** and **almond syrups**, and **cream**. Shake well until smoothly blended, then strain into a wine glass and serve, garnished with a **cherry** on a stick.

Cola Float

Floats have been popular for many years. They're simple to make and fun to drink or eat! Cola drinks are undoubtedly the most popular, but other fizzy drinks are worth trying too.

1 scoop vanilla ice cream
1 can chilled cola

Place the ice cream in the bottom of a tall glass and top up with the cola. Serve with a thick straw and long-handled spoon. Half the fun is scooping out the frothy remains of the ice cream after drinking!

Viennese Coffee

Coffee and dark chocolate conjure up a typical Viennese pavement café scene. This combination makes a delicious after-dinner drink and is a good substitute for an Irish coffee.

1 cup cold, strong black coffee
2 generous Tbsp double cream, plus extra for topping
1 Tbsp dark chocolate syrup
Pinch of ground cinnamon

Place the cold coffee, cream and chocolate syrup in a blender and whisk to a smooth consistency. Pour into a large wine glass, place a dollop of cream on top and sprinkle with the ground cinnamon before serving.

Surfers' Paradise

This is the perfect summer drink, originally designed to be enjoyed after an exhilarating session in the waves, but why wait until the surf is up?

Crushed ice
Juice of 1 fresh lime
2 dashes of Angostura bitters
Lemonade
Slice of orange, to garnish

Place a scoop of crushed ice in a highball glass and pour the lime juice, bitters and lemonade over it. Stir gently and decorate with a slice of orange.

Pom-pom

An egg white gives a drink an attractive silvery sheen and a topping of froth. This drink is best avoided by pregnant women and the elderly.

Ice cubes
1 egg white
1 tsp grenadine
Juice of 1 large lemon
Chilled lemonade

Place six ice cubes in a cocktail shaker, add the egg white, grenadine and lemon juice and shake well. Strain into a tall glass, top up with lemonade and stir gently before serving.

Cairns Cooler

This fruity drink, which originated in Australia, has a distinctively tropical flavour.

Ice cubes
1 part canned pineapple juice
1 part fresh orange juice
½ part coconut cream
1 bar measure of sugar syrup (about an egg cup)
Thin slice of pineapple and maraschino cherry, to garnish

Place about six ice cubes in a cocktail shaker, add the pineapple and orange juices, coconut cream and sugar syrup, and shake well. Strain into a highball glass and garnish with a slice of pineapple, if available, and a cherry on a stick.

Passion

This is a fresh-flavoured and very seductive fruit drink that should be a favourite whenever the fresh juice is available.

1 banana
Juice of 1 orange, mixed with an equal quantity of mango juice
2 dessertspoons passion fruit pulp
Ice cubes
Maraschino cherry, to garnish

Cut the banana into chunks and place in a blender. Add the orange and mango juices, and passion fruit pulp and blend for about 10 seconds. Fill a highball glass with ice cubes and pour the fruit juice mix over it. Garnish with a cherry on a stick.

Fantasia

This delicious drink is rather like a liquid fruit salad
and could easily be served as a dessert
as well as a cocktail.

6 strawberries, rinsed and hulled
Slice of honeydew melon, rind removed
1 part fresh orange juice
1 part pineapple juice
½ part crushed ice
Thin slice of pineapple, to garnish

Place five of the **strawberries**, the **melon**,
and the **orange** and **pineapple juices** in
a blender and blend to a smooth consistency.
Place the **crushed ice** in a highball glass and
pour the blended mixture over it. Garnish with
the remaining strawberry, sliced in half and a
slice of pineapple, if available.

Rock Shandy

This is an old classic and a perfect drink for those occasions when you don't want alcohol, but need to sip something long and refreshing. It's dry enough to appeal to adult tastes, and the dash of bitters gives it a sophisticated look.

Ice cubes
Soda water
Clear lemonade
2 dashes of Angostura bitters
Slice of lemon, to garnish

Place three to four ice cubes in a tall glass, pour in the soda water and lemonade in equal quantities to fill the glass. Stir gently and add a couple of dashes of bitters, allowing it to float near the top and create an attractive band of pink. Garnish with a lemon slice and serve.

Cappucine

This is a sophisticated little drink that's ideal for after dinner, with a mint cream chocolate.

4 parts single cream
1 part peppermint cordial or syrup
Crushed ice
Grated dark chocolate, to serve

Place the **cream** and **peppermint cordial** in a cocktail shaker with a scoop of **crushed ice**. Shake well and strain into a wine glass. Sprinkle a little **grated dark chocolate** over the top and serve.

Grecian Lady

This is one of those fruit-based drinks that can be decorated with any fresh fruit that's in season. It looks exotic and tastes wonderful.

Crushed ice
4 parts peach juice
2 parts orange juice
1 part fresh lemon juice
Soda water
Fruit slices or stoned cherries, to garnish

Place a scoop of crushed ice in a cocktail shaker and add the peach, orange and lemon juices. Shake well and strain into a large wine glass. Add a squirt of soda water to fill the glass and decorate with slices of fruit or stoned cherries threaded on a cocktail stick.

Fizzy Lemonade

One of the oldest drinks in the book, this is always popular as it is refreshing without being cloying or sticky.

Juice of 1 large lemon
2 tsp caster sugar
Soda water
Ice cubes
Slice of lemon, to garnish

Pour the lemon juice into a tall glass, add the sugar and stir until it has dissolved. Top up with soda water and add a few ice cubes, stir gently and garnish with a slice of lemon before serving.

Lemon Ice Cream Soda

This is another old favourite that's
stood the test of time.

Juice of 1 large lemon
2 tsp caster sugar
Soda water
Scoop of soft vanilla ice cream

Pour the **lemon juice** into a tall glass, add the
sugar and stir until it has dissolved. Add **soda
water** to fill the glass to about two-thirds,
stir gently and add a scoop of **ice cream**.
Serve with a thick straw and long-handled spoon.

Mickey Mouse

This merry drink is equally at home
as a mocktail or a dessert.

Ice cubes
Cola
Scoop of vanilla ice cream
Whipped cream
2 maraschino cherries

Place four or five **ice cubes** in a tall glass
and pour the **cola** over them. Add a scoop of
ice cream, then top with **whipped cream** and
decorate with a couple of **cherries**. Serve with
a thick straw and long-handled spoon.

Horse Feathers

For those who prefer a savoury drink rather than a sweet one, this oddly named classic could become a favourite. It can even be served as a starter for a summer meal.

Ice cubes
Clear beef consommé, cooled and chilled
Dash of Tabasco sauce
Dash of Worcestershire sauce
Pinch of salt
Squeeze of lemon juice
Celery stick, to garnish

Place four or five ice cubes in a mixing glass or jug, pour the consommé over it and add the Tabasco and Worcestershire sauces, a pinch of salt and the lemon juice to taste. Stir well and strain into a large wine glass. Garnish with a celery stick, which can double as a stirrer.

Parson's Particular

There are several alcohol-free drinks that suggest they should be served to the parson, presumably assuming that the good cleric would not approve of strong drink at the vicarage fête. This drink is best avoided by pregnant women and the elderly.

Ice cubes
1 part fresh lemon juice
2 parts fresh orange juice
1 egg yolk
2 dashes of grenadine
One glacé cherry, to garnish

Place five or six ice cubes in a shaker, add the lemon and orange juices along with the egg yolk and shake well to blend. Strain into a wine glass, add the grenadine and garnish with a cherry on a stick.

The Keelplate

This is a variation of the classic Bloody Mary, with the addition of clam juice (not available everywhere, but a useful addition to the bar stock when it is found).

Crushed ice
2 parts tomato juice
1 part clam juice
Dash of Worcestershire sauce
Pinch of celery salt
Spring of mint leaves, to garnish

Place a scoop of **crushed ice** in a cocktail shaker and add the **tomato** and **clam juices** along with the **Worcestershire sauce** and **celery salt**. Shake well and strain into a large wine glass. Garnish with **mint leaves** before serving.

Parson's Pleasure

Here's another drink designed to please the vicar. This one is similar to the Parson's Particular, but made as a taller drink. This drink is best avoided by pregnant women and the elderly.

Ice cubes
1 egg yolk
Juice of 1 large orange
4 dashes of grenadine
Soda water
Twist of lemon rind, to garnish

Place five or six ice cubes in a cocktail shaker, add the egg yolk, orange juice and grenadine. Shake well and strain into a tall glass. Top up with soda water and stir gently. Garnish with a twist of lemon and serve.

Saint Clements

Remember the old nursery rhyme about oranges and lemons? That's where this drink found its name.

Crushed ice
1 part fresh orange juice
1 part sparkling bitter lemon
Orange slices, to garnish

Place a scoop of **crushed ice** in a tall glass and add the **orange juice**. Top up with **bitter lemon**, garnish with a slice or two of **orange** and serve.

Red Currant and Lemon Delight

Here's a drink that demonstrates how you can use the most usual ingredients to create delicious drinks. All it takes is a little imagination.

2 Tbsp redcurrant jelly
Boiling water
Ice cubes
Juice of 2 lemons
Soda water
Slice of lemon, to garnish

Place the **redcurrant jelly** in a cup, add an equal quantity of **boiling water** and stir until dissolved. Now place four or five **ice cubes** in a tall glass, pour over the **lemon juice** and add the dissolved jelly. Top up with **soda water** and garnish with a **slice of lemon**.

San Francisco

Here's a delightful tall drink for a hot summer evening. It has all the sweet and tangy flavours of citrus fruits. Pregnant women and the elderly should avoid this drink.

1 part fresh orange juice	Dash of grenadine
1 part grapefruit juice	Ice cubes
1 part fresh lemon juice	Soda water
1 part pineapple juice	Glacé cherries and
1 egg white	Orange slices, to garnish

Place the orange, grapefruit, lemon and pineapple juices along with the egg white and grenadine in a cocktail shaker with five or six ice cubes. Shake well and strain into a tall glass to about the halfway mark. Top up with soda water and garnish with gusto! Use cherries on sticks, slices of orange and anything else that takes your fancy.

Baby Buck

Buck's Fizz is a traditional drink that's popular at Champagne breakfasts. It consists of Champagne and orange juice. There's no reason why you shouldn't replace the Champagne with sparkling grape juice instead. A dash of lime adds a little dryness.

1 part chilled fresh orange juice
1 part sparkling white grape juice
Squeeze of fresh lime juice
Twist of lemon rind, to garnish

Pour the **orange** and **grape juices** in a Champagne flute. Add a squeeze of **lime** and stir gently. Decorate with a **twist of lemon rind** and serve.

Prairie Oyster

This rather interesting drink has long been recommended by some drinkers as the ultimate cure for a hangover, while others say a hangover is more bearable than a Prairie Oyster. The choice is yours. This drink is best avoided by pregnant women and the elderly.

1 egg yolk
Pinch of salt
Dusting of ground black pepper
Dash of Worcestershire sauce
2 drops of Tabasco sauce

Traditionally this drink is **not stirred**.
Simply drop each ingredient into a small wine glass and swallow it in **one gulp**. Frankly, it's slightly more palatable if it is stirred a little.

Southern Belle

The Deep South was the home of the Mint Julep. This is the version originally designed for the younger members of the planter's family — it's a Julep without the alcohol.

2 sprigs of mint leaves
1 tsp caster sugar
Generous squeeze of lemon juice
Ice cubes
Ginger ale

Place a **sprig of mint** in the bottom of a tall glass, add the **sugar** and use a long-handled spoon to crush the two together to extract as much mint flavour as possible. Add a squeeze of **lemon juice**, a few **ice cubes** and top up with **ginger ale**. Garnish with the other sprig of mint and serve, traditionally with a straw.

Summer Soda

This is a good drink to enjoy on a hot summer day round the pool. It looks great and tastes even better.

Juice of 1 orange
Juice of 1 lemon
Juice of 1 grapefruit
Ice cubes
Soda water
Scoop of soft vanilla ice cream
Glacé cherry, to garnish

Pour the **orange, lemon** and **grapefruit juices** in a cocktail shaker with five or six **ice cubes** and shake. Strain into a tall glass, filling it to the halfway mark. Top up to almost full with **soda water** and add a scoop of **vanilla ice cream.** Top with a **cherry** and serve with a straw and long-handled spoon.

Easter Bunny

This deliciously creamy drink is rich and thick
enough to be served as a dessert.

Crushed ice
3 parts frozen natural yoghurt
1 part fresh orange juice
Splash of sugar syrup
Slice of peach, to garnish

Place a scoop of **crushed ice, yoghurt,
orange juice** and **sugar syrup** in a blender
and blend to a smooth consistency.
Pour into a wine goblet and garnish
with a **slice of ripe peach**.

Strawberry Milkshake

This is a quick and easy refreshing drink to make in strawberry season. If using the egg, this drink is best avoided by pregnant women and the elderly.

1 scoop of crushed ice
Equal measure of fresh strawberries,
rinsed and hulled
1 cup whole milk
1 Tbsp runny honey
1 whole egg (optional)

Place the **crushed ice** in a blender and add the **strawberries** (reserving one for the garnish), along with the **milk**, **honey**, and **egg**, if using. Blend until creamy smooth and top with half a strawberry. Serve with a thick straw.

Chocolate Malt

This is always a favourite with chocolate lovers.
It was a universal favourite in the days
of the drive-in roadside café.

1 part soft chocolate ice cream
3 parts whole milk, well chilled
Generous squeeze of chocolate syrup
2 dessertspoons malt powder
Chocolate vermicelli

Place all the ingredients (minus the
chocolate vermicelli) into a blender and
blend until smooth. Pour into a tall glass,
sprinkle a topping of chocolate vermicelli
and serve with a thick straw.

Rosie's Ruby Heart

I have no idea who Rosie was, but she obviously had a kind heart for somebody to name a drink after her. This is a good one to have ready for the strawberry season. The freshest fruit always makes the tastiest drinks.

Crushed ice
6 fresh strawberries, rinsed and hulled
Equal volume of single cream
2 Tbsp (or to taste) sour mix (see page 23)

Place a scoop of **crushed ice** in a blender and add the **strawberries** (reserving one for the garnish), **cream** and **sour mix**. Blend until smooth and serve, garnished with the remaining strawberry.

Orange 'n' Bitters

Drinks do not have to be complicated to be good.
This one simply uses the tangy bitterness of
Angostura bitters to add a new dimension to plain
fresh orange juice.

Crushed ice
2 dashes of Angostura bitters
1 glass chilled fresh orange juice
Sprig of mint, to garnish

Fill a highball glass with **crushed ice**, add a
couple of dashes of **bitters** and fill with
orange juice. Garnish with a **sprig of mint**
and serve with a straw.

The Limey

British sailors earned the nickname 'limeys' because they were served regular doses of lime juice in order to combat scurvy during long ocean voyages. This one should set your boat rocking! This drink is best avoided by pregnant women and the elderly.

Ice cubes
1 part fresh lemon juice
2 parts fresh lime juice
1 egg white
Maraschino cherry, to garnish

Place five or six ice cubes in a cocktail shaker, add the lemon and lime juices and the egg white. Shake well to blend together and strain into a Martini glass. Garnish with a cherry on a cocktail stick.

Soda and Bitters

If you want a quite austere drink without any sticky sweetness, this one could be just for you.

Ice cubes
Couple of dashed of Angostura bitters
Soda water

Fill a highball glass with ice cubes, add a couple of dashes of bitters, top up with soda water and serve ungarnished.

Sober Moment

This is a classic blend of flavours, with the slightly bitter tonic water balancing the other sweet tastes.

Ice cubes
1 part fresh orange juice
1 part fresh lime juice
Splash of grenadine
Tonic water
Twist of lime rind, to garnish

Fill a highball glass with ice cubes, add the orange and lime juices and trickle the splash of grenadine over it before topping up the glass with tonic water. Garnish with a twist of lime rind and serve.

Safe Sex on the Beach

The original Sex on the Beach cocktail is made with vodka and Midori liqueur. This one, as the name suggests, is the safe version, but still a sexy drink.

Ice cubes
1 part peach nectar
(concentrated frozen peach juice)
3 parts fresh orange juice
3 parts grapefruit juice
(or pineapple juice if you prefer)
Slice of fresh peach, to garnish

Fill a highball glass with ice cubes and pour in the peach nectar, orange and grapefruit juices. Stir gently and garnish with a slice of peach before serving.

Mexican Sunset

This is a safe variation of the traditional
Tequila Sunset, which obviously relies
on fiery tequila for its kick.

Ice cubes
Juice of 2 oranges
1 Tbsp grenadine
Chunk of pineapple and a glacé cherry, to garnish

Fill a wine glass or whisky glass with ice cubes
and pour the orange juice over them. Now
carefully float the grenadine on top of it, trying
to keep the colours separate. The best way to
do this is to trickle the liquid carefully over
the back of a spoon on to the layer beneath it.
Serve garnished with a chunk of pineapple
and a cherry on a cocktail stick.

Virgin Margarita

The alcoholic Margarita has become a very trendy cocktail, getting its sour flavour from lemon juice and its kick from tequila, so this safe version should have wide appeal.

Lemon and salt, for frosting
3 parts sour mix (see page 23)
1 part lime cordial
1 part fresh orange juice
Crushed ice

Frost the rim of a wine goblet or cocktail glass by rubbing it all around with a halved lemon and dipping it into a saucer of salt. Shake the sour mix, lime cordial and orange juice in a cocktail shaker with a scoop of crushed ice and strain carefully into the frosted glass. Serve with a short straw.

Virgin Pina Colada

Here's another popular tropical drink in a more sober guise. Shop around for the coconut cream. It makes all the difference if you can find it.

Crushed ice
5 or 6 pineapple chunks, if available
1 part pineapple juice
Generous splash of fresh orange juice
1 part coconut cream
1 Tbsp single cream
Maraschino cherry, to garnish

Place a scoop of crushed ice in a blender and add the pineapple chunks, pineapple and orange juices along with the coconut cream and single cream. Blend for about 10 seconds, then strain into a red wine goblet. Decorate with a cherry on a cocktail stick and serve with a straw.

Virgin Sea Breeze

This tangy and refreshing drink evokes
dreams of warm tropical beaches.
It's very easy and quick to make.

Ice cubes
1 part cranberry juice
1 part grapefruit juice

Fill a highball glass with ice cubes,
pour the cranberry and grapefruit juices
over the ice, stir gently and serve ungarnished.

Royal Fizz

The original cocktail of this name contains raspberry brandy. Here it's made with raspberry syrup instead and it's just as pleasant. A perfect drink for a hot summer's day.

Cracked ice
1 part fresh orange juice
1 part lime cordial
1 part raspberry syrup
Soda water

Place a small scoop of **cracked ice** (ice cubes wrapped in a tea cloth and smacked with a rolling pin or steak mallet) in a cocktail shaker and add the **orange juice, lime cordial** and **raspberry syrup.** Shake well and strain into a tall glass. Top up with chilled **soda water** and serve with a straw.

Yankee Flip

This is another standard cocktail recipe that has converted comfortably into a mocktail. The original contained red wine. Here we used red grape juice and it works just as well. Pregnant women and the elderly should not be served this drink.

Ice cubes
1 egg yolk
1 tsp caster sugar
1 part pineapple juice
2 parts red grape juice
Grated nutmeg, to serve

Place five or six ice cubes in a cocktail shaker and add the egg yolk, sugar, pineapple and grape juices. Shake thoroughly until smoothly blended and strain into a wine glass. Grate a sprinkling of nutmeg over it and serve.

Grape Sparkler

This is an attractive drink to serve during the grape harvest, when grapes are plentiful. The original recipe calls for Champagne instead of grape juice.

2 whole white grapes
2 whole black grapes
Squeeze of lemon juice
Sparkling white grape juice, well chilled

Thread the **white** and **black grapes** alternately on a long cocktail stick and stand it upright in a Champagne flute. Squeeze a little **lemon juice** over them and fill the glass with **sparkling grape juice**.

Silver Sour

The egg whites give this little drink a nice gloss and the lemon juice provides a tangy balance to the sweetness of the apricot juice. This drink is best avoided by pregnant women and the elderly.

1 egg white
Ice cubes
Juice of 1 large lemon
Equal quantity of thick apricot juice or purée
1 tsp caster sugar
Soda water
2 slices of green apple, to garnish

Place the egg white in a cocktail shaker with four ice cubes, the lemon juice and apricot juice or purée. Add the sugar (or adjust to taste) and shake well for about 10 seconds. Strain into a wine goblet and top up with soda water. Stir gently and decorate with a couple of slices of apple on the rim of the glass.

Daddy's Darling

This very sweet and attractive drink falls somewhere between being a mocktail and a dessert. It's a treat for anybody with a sweet tooth.

1 part cherry-flavoured syrup
1 part sweetened condensed milk
1 scoop of vanilla ice cream
Soda water
1 scoop of raspberry ice cream
Whipped cream and pineapple chunks, to garnish

Pour the cherry syrup and condensed milk into a tall glass and mix together. Carefully add the vanilla ice cream, then add soda water to about two-thirds of the glass. Now top with a scoop of raspberry ice cream and decorate with a dollop of whipped cream and pineapple chunks. Serve with a thick straw and long-handled spoon.

Very Lemony Ade

This is a deliciously refreshing drink for those who like their lemonade with more lemon sourness and less sweetness.

Ice cubes
Generous splash of sour mix (see page 23)
Soda water
Sparkling bitter lemon
Twist of lemon, to garnish

Fill a tall glass with **ice cubes** and pour the **sour mix** over them. Add the **soda water** and **bitter lemon** in equal quantities to fill the glass, stir gently and garnish with a **twist of lemon**. Serve with a straw.

Ginger Snap

Anybody who enjoys ginger beer will appreciate the flick of ginger heat in this unusual drink. If you can't find ginger marmalade, you could substitute lime marmalade and add a little more ginger.

Crushed ice
1 part fresh orange juice
1 part grapefruit juice
1 part cranberry juice
2 tsp ginger marmalade
½ tsp ground ginger or fresh grated ginger root
Slice of orange, to garnish

Place a scoop of **crushed ice** in a cocktail shaker and add the **orange, grapefruit** and **cranberry juices, ginger marmalade** and the **ground** or **grated ginger**. Shake well, strain into a tall glass and garnish with a **slice of orange**.

Ginger Peach Shake

By reducing the quantity of milk and increasing the ice cream, this delicious fruit-based shake could be turned into a super dessert.

1 large, fresh peach, peeled and cut into chunks
(or the equivalent quantity of canned peaches)
Chilled whole milk
2 scoops of vanilla or peach ice cream
¼ tsp ground ginger
¼ tsp powdered cinnamon
Whipped cream

Place the **peach chunks** in a blender with two tablespoons of **milk** and blend to a smooth purée. Add the **ice cream** and about a cup of milk, along with the **ginger** and **cinnamon**. Blend until smooth, pour into a tall glass and top with a dollop of **whipped cream**. Serve with a thick straw.

Jones Beach Cocktail

This savoury drink uses lemon juice to balance the saltiness of the beef consommé. To make consommé, dissolve a beef stock cube in a cup of boiling water.

Crushed ice
1 cup beef consommé, cooled
Half the quantity of clam juice
Juice of ½ lemon (or lime)
½ tsp horseradish sauce
Couple of dashed of Worcestershire sauce
Celery salt
Sprig of parsley, to garnish

Place a scoop of **crushed ice** in a cocktail shaker and add all the ingredients until well mixed. Now place two **ice cubes** in a tall glass and strain the blended drink over them. Serve ungarnished or with a **sprig of parsley**.

Choc-nut Sundae Sipper

Enthusiastic drink mixers try all kinds of unusual ingredients — who would have thought of adding peanut butter to a milkshake?

1 generous Tbsp crunchy peanut butter
Equal quantity of chocolate syrup
About 1 cup whole milk
2 scoops chocolate or pecan nut ice cream
Whipped cream and chopped nuts, to serve

Place the **peanut butter**, **chocolate syrup** and a little **milk** into a blender and blend until smooth. Add the remaining milk and the **ice cream** and blend again for three or four seconds. Pour into a tall glass, top with a dollop of **whipped cream** and sprinkle with **chopped nuts**.

Note: Please ensure that your guests do not have nut allergies before serving this drink.

Plum Joy

Using fresh fruit or freshly squeezed juice always adds to the flavour of a drink. Canned or preserved fruit products are fine, but they do lack the pure tang of fresh fruit.

2 large, very ripe plums
Crushed ice
Juice of ½ lemon
2 Tbsp sugar syrup (see page 23)
2 Tbsp plum jam
Sparkling bitter lemon

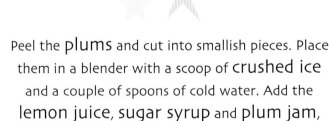

Peel the plums and cut into smallish pieces. Place them in a blender with a scoop of crushed ice and a couple of spoons of cold water. Add the lemon juice, sugar syrup and plum jam, and blend to a smooth purée. Strain this into a tall glass and top up with the bitter lemon. Stir gently to blend and serve.

Jungle Cooler

You're usually safe when you combine different fruit juices. There are very few combinations that don't go well together. This one was designed to capture the exotic character of the tropical jungle.

Crushed ice
4 parts pineapple juice
2 parts fresh orange juice
1 part passion fruit squash or cordial
1 part coconut milk
Slice of pineapple, to garnish

Place a scoop of **crushed ice** in a cocktail shaker and add the **pineapple, orange** and **passion fruit juices** along with the **coconut milk**.
Shake well and strain into a tall glass.
Garnish with a **slice of pineapple** and serve.

Blue Spark

There are few things as dramatic — or unexpected — as a blue drink. I created this one for a corporate dinner for a company whose logo was blue. Most of the staff were teetotallers, so alcohol was not acceptable in the blend. It went down very well.

Crushed ice
½ tsp blue food colouring
2 dashes of Angostura bitters
1 part lychee juice
3 parts fizzy lemonade
Slice of lemon, to garnish

Place a scoop of **crushed ice** into a tall mixing glass or small jug. Add the **food colouring**, **bitters** and **lychee juice**. Add the **lemonade** and stir gently so as not to lose the fizz. Strain into a large highball glass and garnish with a **slice of lemon**.

Fruit Cup

This is one of those useful drinks that can be made as a single cocktail or a large fruit punch, served in a punch bowl with fruit pieces floating on top.

Ice cubes
1 part fresh orange juice
1 part grapefruit juice
1 part pineapple juice
1 part apple juice

Slices of whatever fruit is available: lemon, orange, kiwi fruit or strawberry, or all of the above, to garnish

To make a single cocktail, place four or five ice cubes into a cocktail shaker, add the orange, grapefruit, pineapple and apple juices and shake well. Strain into a tall glass, decorate with fruit slices and serve with a colourful straw.

Lassie

I'm not sure whether this little drink was named after a Scottish girl or the famous movie dog, but it's a popular old classic among mocktails and has a very appealing flavour.

Ice cubes
4 parts plain drinking yoghurt
1 part double cream
2 tsp caster sugar
Glacé or maraschino cherry, to garnish

Place a scoop of ice cubes in a cocktail shaker, add the yoghurt, cream and caster sugar and shake vigorously. Strain into a Martini glass or wine goblet and garnish with a cherry on a stick.

Honeysweet Coffee

Most cocktails are designed to be enjoyed at sunset or later. This one can be enjoyed at any time — even breakfast.

1 tsp runny honey
1 mug of hot strong black coffee
(preferably not instant coffee)
Ice cubes
Dash of Angostura bitters
Whipped cream and grated nutmeg, to serve

Dissolve the honey in the mug of hot coffee and allow to cool. When ready to serve, place five ice cubes in a cocktail shaker, add the dash of bitters, pour in the cold coffee mixture and shake well. Strain into a tall glass, add a dollop of whipped cream and dust with grated nutmeg before serving.

Catherine Blossom Cocktail

I discovered this drink in Canada, where maple syrup is widely used as a sweetener. It has a delightfully fresh taste.

Crushed ice
Juice of 2 fresh oranges
Juice of ½ small lemon
2 dessertspoons maple syrup
Twist of lemon peel, to garnish

Place a scoop of **crushed ice** in a blender, add the **orange** and **lemon juices** along with the **maple syrup**. Blend well and strain into a wine goblet. Serve garnished with a **twist of lemon peel**.

Cherry Pop

Good cocktails should look as good as they taste. This attractive drink has a good balance of sweet and sour, which you can adjust to suit your palate.

Ice cubes
2 parts cherry syrup
2 parts fresh orange juice
1 part fresh lemon juice
Soda water
Slice of lemon and a glacé cherry, to serve

Place five or six ice cubes in a cocktail shaker, add the cherry syrup, orange and lemon juices and shake well. Strain into a wine goblet, top up with a little soda water and decorate with a slice of lemon and cherry to serve. (For a taller, but less intensely flavoured drink, serve in a tall glass, topped up with much more soda water.)

Honeymoon Cocktail

After all that Champagne at the wedding reception, the bride and groom need something light and fresh. Make two small drinks and serve them in matching glasses.

Crushed ice
1 part apple juice
1 part fresh orange juice
Squeeze of fresh lime juice
2 tsp runny honey
Orange peel and a maraschino cherry, to garnish

Place a scoop of **crushed ice** in a cocktail shaker, add the **apple** and **orange juices**, squeeze over the **lime** and pour in the **honey**. Shake well and strain into two Champagne flutes. Garnish with a spiral of **orange peel** and a **cherry**.

Virgin Lea

This classic cocktail combines a range of flavours happily. You'll find sweetness, tangy sharpness and some spice flavours.

½ yellow pepper (seeds removed)
Crushed ice
2 parts tomato juice
1 part passion fruit juice (or cordial)
1 tsp runny honey
2 dashes of Worcestershire sauce
Cherry tomato, to garnish

Cut the yellow pepper into smallish slices and place them in a blender with a scoop of crushed ice. Add the tomato and passion fruit juices, honey and Worcestershire sauce. Blend thoroughly until the mixture is quite smooth. Strain into a lowball (or whiskey) glass and garnish with a cherry tomato on a stick.

Island Romance

This drink combines tropical flavours in an attractive blend. Try to float each ingredient gently on top of the previous one for a dramatic effect.

1 slice fresh, ripe honeydew melon
Crushed ice
Juice of 1 large orange
Equal quantity of coconut milk
Equal quantity of mango juice
1 Tbsp whipped cream

Peel and cut the melon into chunks. Place the pieces in a blender with a scoop of crushed ice and blend to a purée. Place this carefully into a Champagne flute, filling it to about one third. Now float the coconut milk on top of it, followed by the orange and mango juices, trying to keep them separate (not essential, but it's fun to try!). Top with whipped cream and serve.

Snow Queen

This easy-to-make short drink is very attractive and has a nice sharpness to it. The egg white gives it a silvery froth, so it requires no garnish to make it look pretty. This drink is best avoided by pregnant women and the elderly.

Ice cubes
1 egg white
Generous dash of lime cordial
Lemonade

Place five **ice cubes** in a cocktail shaker and add the **egg white** and a splash of **lime cordial**. Shake very well and strain into a cocktail glass. Carefully top up the glass with **lemonade**, allowing the frothy egg-snow to float on top. Serve ungarnished.

Index

191

Acknowledgements

The publisher would like to thank Denby
(www.denbypottery.co.uk) for supplying glasses and tableware
for photography.